Complete
Sonatas for Violin and Piano

Edvard Grieg

DOVER PUBLICATIONS, INC.
Mineola, New York

Bibliographical Note

This Dover edition, first published in 1998, is a new compilation of three works originally published separately. C. F. Peters, Leipzig, originally published *Sonate für Pianoforte
und Violine von Edvard Grieg, Op. 8,* as Edition Peters No. 1340, n.d. G. Schirmer, New
York, originally published *Edvard Grieg / Op. 13 / Sonata for Piano and Violin (No. II) in
G,* and *Op. 45 / Sonata for Piano and Violin (No. III) in C Minor* as Volumes 524 (1901)
and 981 (1910), respectively, of Schirmer's Library of Musical Classics, "edited and fingered
by Leopold Lichtenberg." A composite list of contents and headings are newly added.

We are indebted to the Music Library, Cornell University, New York, for their loan of the
scores for this edition.

International Standard Book Number: 0-486-40233-9

Manufactured in the United States of America
Dover Publications, Inc., 31 East 2nd Street, Mineola, N.Y. 11501

CONTENTS

THREE SONATAS FOR VIOLIN AND PIANO

To Mr. August Fries

Sonata in F Major
Op. 8 (1865)

Sonata in F Major
Op. 8

I.

Allegro con brio.

più animato

II. Allegretto quasi Andantino.

III. Allegro molto vivace.

To Johán S. Svendsen

Sonata in G Major
Op. 13 (1867)

Sonata in G Major

Op. 13

Edited and fingered by Leopold Lichtenberg

I.

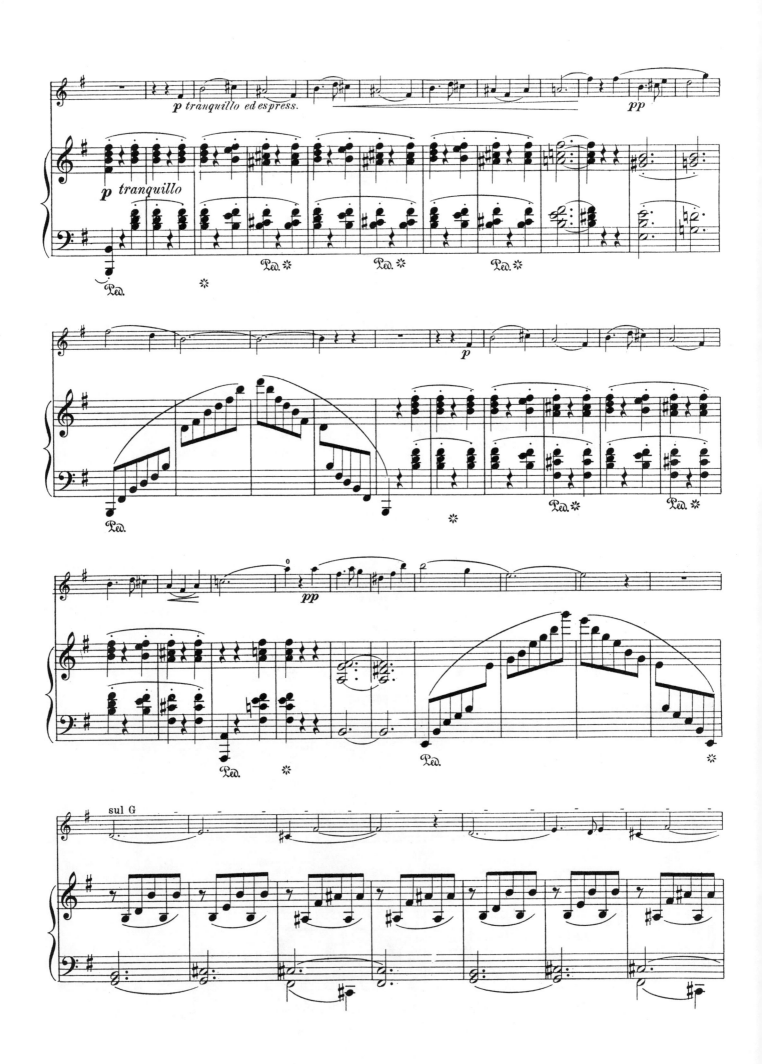

II.

III.

VIOLIN

Complete
Sonatas for Violin and Piano

Edvard Grieg

DOVER PUBLICATIONS, INC.
Mineola, New York

CONTENTS

THREE SONATAS FOR VIOLIN AND PIANO

Bibliographical Note

This Dover edition, first published in 1998, is a new compilation of three works originally published separately. C. F. Peters, Leipzig, originally published *Sonate für Pianoforte und Violine von Edvard Grieg, Op. 8,* as Edition Peters No. 1340, n.d. G. Schirmer, New York, originally published *Edvard Grieg / Op. 13 / Sonata for Piano and Violin (No. II) in G,* and *Op. 45 / Sonata for Piano and Violin (No. III) in C Minor* as Volumes 524 (1901) and 981 (1910), respectively, of Schirmer's Library of Musical Classics, "edited and fingered by Leopold Lichtenberg." A composite list of contents and headings are newly added.

We are indebted to the Music Library, Cornell University, New York, for their loan of the scores for this edition.

International Standard Book Number: 0-486-40233-9

Manufactured in the United States of America
Dover Publications, Inc., 31 East 2nd Street, Mineola, N.Y. 11501

To Mr. August Fries

Sonata in F Major
Op. 8 (1865)

I.

II.

To Johán S. Svendsen

Sonata in G Major
Op. 13 (1867)

Edited and fingered by Leopold Lichtenberg

II.

16   *Sonata, Op. 13*

III.

Allegro animato.

Sonata in C Minor

Op. 45 (1886–7)

I.

Edited and fingered by Leopold Lichtenberg

Allegro molto ed appassionato (♩. = 116)

II.

Allegretto espressivo alla Romanza (♩ = 72)

III.

To Franz von Lendbach

Sonata in C Minor
Op. 45 (1886–7)

Sonata in C Minor
Op. 45

Edited and fingered by Leopold Lichtenberg

I.

Allegro molto ed appassionato (♩. = 116)

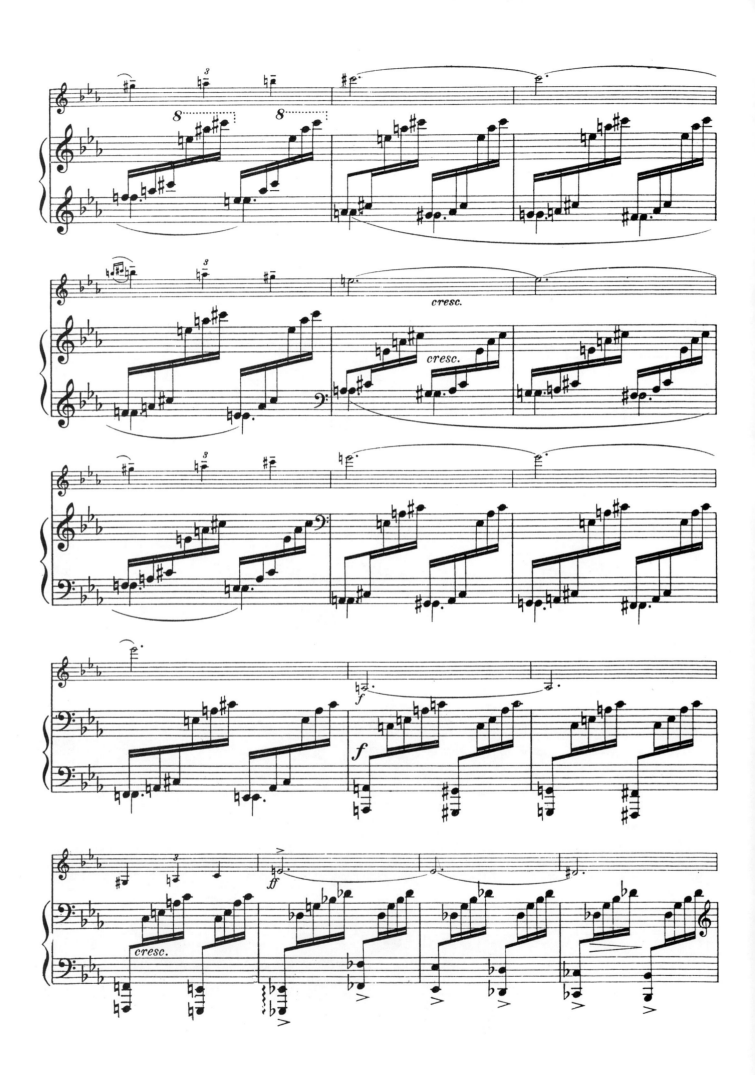

II.

Allegretto espressivo alla Romanza (♩= 72)

Allegro molto (♩=80)

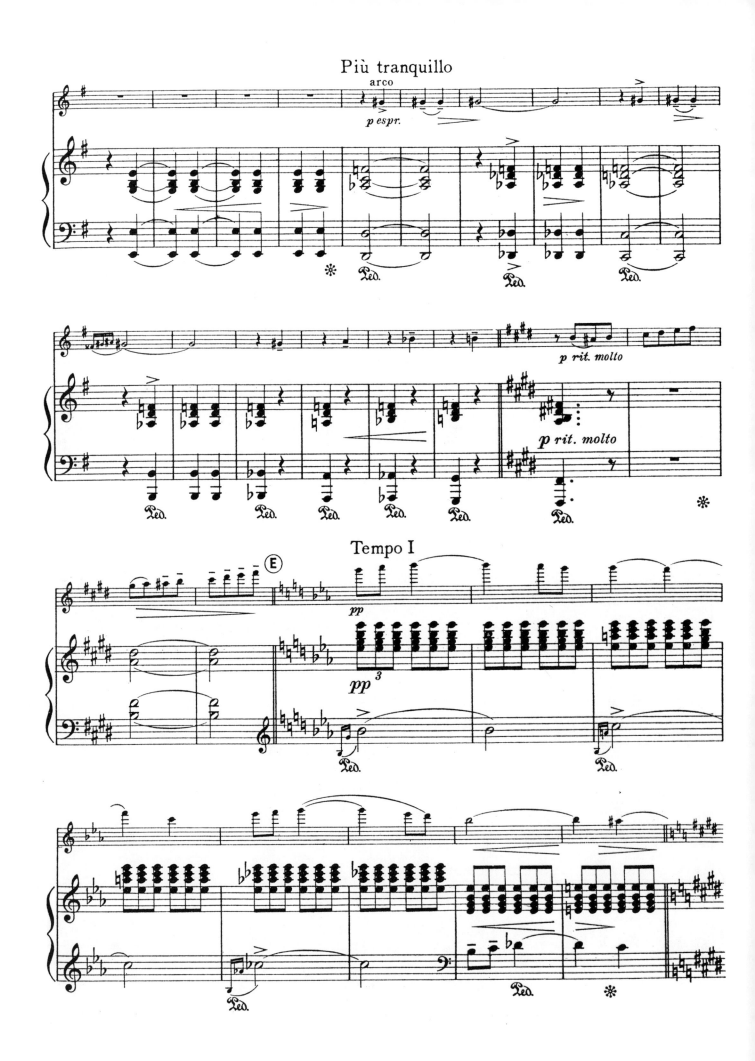

III.

Allegro animato ($\mathbf{\downarrow = 104}$)

Dover Chamber Music Scores

COMPLETE SUITES FOR UNACCOMPANIED CELLO AND SONATAS FOR VIOLA DA GAMBA, Johann Sebastian Bach. Bach-Gesellschaft edition of the six cello suites (BWV 1007–1012) and three sonatas (BWV 1027–1029), commonly played today on the cello. 112pp. 9⅜ × 12¼. 25641-3 Pa. **$8.95**

WORKS FOR VIOLIN, Johann Sebastian Bach. Complete Sonatas and Partitas for Unaccompanied Violin; Six Sonatas for Violin and Clavier. Bach-Gesellschaft edition. 158pp. 9⅜ × 12¼. 23683-8 Pa. **$9.95**

COMPLETE STRING QUARTETS, Wolfgang Amadeus Mozart. Breitkopf & Härtel edition. All 23 string quartets plus alternate slow movement to K.156. Study score. 277pp. 9⅜ × 12¼. 22372-8 Pa. **$13.95**

COMPLETE STRING QUINTETS, Wolfgang Amadeus Mozart. All the standard-instrumentation string quintets, plus String Quintet in C Minor, K.406; Quintet with Horn or Second Cello, K.407; and Clarinet Quintet, K.581. Breitkopf & Härtel edition. Study score. 181pp. 9⅜ × 12¼. 23603-X Pa. **$9.95**

STRING QUARTETS, OPP. 20 and 33, COMPLETE, Joseph Haydn. Complete reproductions of the 12 masterful quartets (six each) of Opp. 20 and 33–in the reliable Eulenburg edition. 272pp. 8⅜ × 11¼. 24852-6 Pa. **$12.95**

STRING QUARTETS, OPP. 42, 50 and 54, Joseph Haydn. Complete reproductions of Op. 42 in D Minor; Op. 50, Nos. 1–6 ("Prussian Quartets") and Op. 54, Nos. 1–3. Reliable Eulenburg edition. 224pp. 8⅜ × 11¼. 24262-5 Pa. **$12.95**

TWELVE STRING QUARTETS, Joseph Haydn. 12 often-performed works: Op. 55, Nos. 1–3 (including *Razor*); Op. 64, Nos. 1–6; Op. 71, Nos. 1–3. Definitive Eulenburg edition. 288pp. 8⅜ × 11¼. 23933-0 Pa. **$13.95**

ELEVEN LATE STRING QUARTETS, Joseph Haydn. Complete reproductions of Op. 74, Nos. 1–3; Op. 76, Nos. 1–6; and Op. 77, Nos. 1 and 2. Definitive Eulenburg edition. Full-size study score. 320pp. 8⅜ × 11¼. 23753-2 Pa. **$13.95**

COMPLETE STRING QUARTETS, Ludwig van Beethoven. Breitkopf & Härtel edition. Six quartets of Opus 18; three quartets of Opus 59; Opera 74, 95, 127, 130, 131, 132, 135 and Grosse Fuge. Study score. 434pp. 9⅜ × 12¼. 22361-2 Pa. **$16.95**

SIX GREAT PIANO TRIOS IN FULL SCORE, Ludwig van Beethoven. Definitive Breitkopf & Härtel edition of Beethoven's Piano Trios Nos. 1–6 including the "Ghost" and the "Archduke." 224pp. 9⅜ × 12¼. 25398-8 Pa. **$11.95**

COMPLETE VIOLIN SONATAS, Ludwig van Beethoven. All ten sonatas including the "Kreutzer" and "Spring" sonatas in the definitive Breitkopf & Härtel edition. 256pp. 9 × 12. 26277-4 Pa. **$13.95**

COMPLETE SONATAS AND VARIATIONS FOR CELLO AND PIANO, Ludwig van Beethoven. All five sonatas and three sets of variations. Reprinted from Breitkopf & Härtel edition. 176pp. 9⅜ × 12¼. 26441-6 Pa. **$10.95**

COMPLETE CHAMBER MUSIC FOR STRINGS, Franz Schubert. Reproduced from famous Breitkopf & Härtel edition: Quintet in C Major (1828), 15 quartets and two trios for violin(s), viola, and violincello. Study score. 348pp. 9 × 12. 21463-X Pa. **$15.95**

CAPRICE VIENNOIS AND OTHER FAVORITE PIECES FOR VIOLIN AND PIANO: With Separate Violin Part, Fritz Kreisler. *Liebesfreud, Liebesleid, Schön Rosmarin, Sicilienne and Rigaudon,* more. 64pp. plus slip-in violin part. 9 × 12. (Available in U.S. only) 28489-1 Pa. **$7.95**

COMPLETE CHAMBER MUSIC FOR PIANOFORTE AND STRINGS, Franz Schubert. Breitkopf & Härtel edition. *Trout,* Quartet in F Major, and trios for piano, violin, cello. Study score. 192pp. 9 × 12. 21527-X Pa. **$11.95**

CHAMBER WORKS FOR PIANO AND STRINGS, Felix Mendelssohn. Eleven of the composer's best known works in the genre–duos, trios, quartets and a sextet–reprinted from authoritative Breitkopf & Härtel edition. 384pp. 9⅜ × 12¼. 26117-4 Pa. **$19.95**

COMPLETE CHAMBER MUSIC FOR STRINGS, Felix Mendelssohn. All of Mendelssohn's chamber music: Octet, Two Quintets, Six Quartets, and Four Pieces for String Quartet. (Nothing with piano is included.) Complete works edition (1874–7). Study score. 283pp. 9⅜ × 12¼. 23679-X Pa. **$13.95**

CHAMBER MUSIC OF ROBERT SCHUMANN, edited by Clara Schumann. Superb collection of three trios, four quartets, and piano quintet. Breitkopf & Härtel edition. 288pp. 9⅜ × 12¼. 24101-7 Pa. **$14.95**

COMPLETE SONATAS FOR SOLO INSTRUMENT AND PIANO, Johannes Brahms. All seven sonatas–three for violin, two for cello and two for clarinet (or viola)–reprinted from the authoritative Breitkopf & Härtel edition. 208pp. 9 × 12. 26091-7 Pa. **$12.95**

COMPLETE CHAMBER MUSIC FOR STRINGS AND CLARINET QUINTET, Johannes Brahms. Vienna Gesellschaft der Musikfreunde edition of all quartets, quintets, and sextet without piano. Study edition. 262pp. 8⅜ × 11¼. 21914-3 Pa. **$12.95**

QUINTET AND QUARTETS FOR PIANO AND STRINGS, Johannes Brahms. Full scores of *Quintet in F Minor,* Op. 34; *Quartet in G Minor,* Op. 25; *Quartet in A Major,* Op. 26; *Quartet in C Minor,* Op. 60. Breitkopf & Härtel edition. 298pp. 9 × 12. 24900-X Pa. **$15.95**

COMPLETE PIANO TRIOS, Johannes Brahms. All five piano trios in the definitive Breitkopf & Härtel edition. 288pp. 9 × 12. 25769-X Pa. **$14.95**

CHAMBER WORKS FOR PIANO AND STRINGS, Antonín Dvořák. Society editions of the F Minor and Dumky piano trios, D Major and E-flat Major piano quartets and A Major piano quintet. 352pp. 8⅜ × 11¼. (Available in U.S. only) 25663-4 Pa. **$15.95**

FIVE LATE STRING QUARTETS, Antonín Dvořák. Treasury of Czech master's finest chamber works: Nos. 10, 11, 12, 13, 14. Reliable Simrock editions. 282pp. 8¼ × 11. 25135-7 Pa. **$12.95**

STRING QUARTETS BY DEBUSSY AND RAVEL/Claude Debussy: Quartet in G Minor, Op. 10/Maurice Ravel: Quartet in F Major, Claude Debussy and Maurice Ravel. Authoritative one-volume edition of two influential masterpieces noted for individuality, delicate and subtle beauties. 112pp. 8¼ × 11. (Not available in France or Germany) 25231-0 Pa. **$7.95**

GREAT CHAMBER WORKS, César Franck. Four great works: Violin Sonata in A Major, Piano Trio in F-sharp Minor, String Quartet in D Major and Piano Quintet in F Minor. From J. Hamelle, Paris and C. F. Peters, Leipzig editions. 248pp. 9⅜ × 12¼. 26546-3 Pa. **$13.95**

COMPLETE STRING QUARTETS, Peter Ilyitch Tchaikovsky and Alexander Borodin. Tchaikovsky's Quartets Nos. 1–3 and Borodin's Quartets Nos. 1 and 2 reproduced from authoritative editions. 240pp. 8⅜ × 11¼. 28333-X Pa. **$12.95**

Available from your music dealer or write for free Music Catalog to
Dover Publications, Inc., Dept. MUBI, 31 East 2nd Street, Mineola, N.Y. 11501.